A-Z OF GOOD GOVERNANCE

By Bill Crooks and Jackie Mouradian

Written and illustrated by Bill Crooks and Jackie Mouradian
Graphic design: Lindsay Noble

Mosaic Creative
www.mosaiccreative.co.uk
info@mosaiccreative.co.uk
+44 (0) 118 9611359

First edition 2012

© 2012 Mosaic Creative. All rights reserved.
ISBN #: 978-1-4716-1379-1

Mosaic Creative are committed to using the visual and performing arts in providing fun and accessible training and resources for the voluntary sector in the UK and overseas.

"I hope that, over the course of the next few years, we'll see charities viewing good governance not as a hurdle to clear, but as an opportunity to show the public they're accountable, they're trustworthy, they're a wise investment. Think of your relationship with the public as a contract in good faith, not as a relationship of unconditional love."

Sam Younger
Chief Executive of the Charity Commission
June 2011

How to use the A-Z of Good Governance

This booklet includes simple illustrated explanations of some of the terms used in governance. It includes questions or exercises aimed at helping you and your organisation reflect on how you operate as a board.

You might like to use the ideas and activities in this book in your board meetings for training trustees, or discuss one page per week at your office in a tea break. Alternatively, use the book as part of an away day activity for developing your board.

Is for... Accountability

Accountability is where a person or an organisation is expected to explain their decisions and actions to others.

You can think of accountability as being two sides of a coin. Your organisation has a moral accountability to the people you serve, the people who fund your work and your staff who work for you.

The flipside is the legal side which might include producing annual reports, financial audits, keeping to health and safety or child protection laws.

2 SIDES OF THE COIN

Things to think about

1. Make a list of all the people you think you are accountable to.
2. Decide which people you are legally accountable to and which people you are morally accountable to.
3. In what ways are we demonstrating how we are accountable to these different groups? Are these effective?

A-Z Of Good Governance

B

Is for... Board

**What do you call yours?
A committee? A council?**

The board is the governing body of a voluntary or community organisation. The people that make up the board should have a good range of different skills, knowledge and experience, which when combined can be used to steer the organisation effectively.

Questions

1. What do we most value about being a board member and how do we appreciate each other?
2. How many people serve on our board? Is this too many, too few or about right?
3. Do we have the right skills and experience to help us work effectively?

C

Is for... Chair

What is the role of the chair?

- To provide leadership and direction to the board, enabling them to carry out their roles effectively for the good of the organisation.
- To help the board set long term plans for the future of the organisation.
- To run the meetings, approve the agenda, ensure good participation and decision-making and help the board work as a team.
- To work alongside the chief officer in ensuring that the decisions of the board members are acted upon.

Questions

1. What does our board need from its chair?
2. What kind of leadership does this organisation and board need from the chair?
3. How can we support our chair in their leadership role?

A-Z Of Good Governance

D
Is for... Delegation

Make a list of typical tasks that are delegated in your organisation.

How well are they delegated? – is there enough explanation about what is involved?

Are we burdening some people and under-using others?

What can we do to improve the way in which tasks are delegated so that they can be completed effectively?

More thoughts on delegation

The board cannot run the organisation alone – it must delegate some authority and responsibility to the organisation's staff and volunteers, subcommittees and working groups, through the chief officer if there is one. Some may be tempted to delegate the things they don't want to be involved with. However the person who delegates the task is responsible for seeing the task carried through. Delegation is about sharing the burden, not giving up ownership.

A-Z Of Good Governance

Is for...
Equality and diversity

A diverse board will:

- Be more responsive to the community it serves.
- Bring fresh perspectives to the way the organisation is governed.
- Be more inclusive in the way its mission is fulfilled.

Questions

1. How could your board be more representative of people from different ethnic and cultural backgrounds, people with disabilities and young people?
2. How can your board value and celebrate the contribution of people from diverse groups?
3. What contribution could a more diverse board make to the success of the organisation?

A-Z Of Good Governance

F

Is for... Fruit Tree

Think of your organisation as parts of a tree. Which parts of the tree represent the different aspects of your organisation –

- roots?
- trunk?
- branches?
- leaves?
- fruit?

FRUIT
what are we achieving?

BRANCHES/LEAVES
what projects/activities are we working on?

TRUNK
how are we organised – board, staff, volunteers?

ROOTS
what are our values and what are we about?

A-Z Of Good Governance

G

Is for... Governance

Governance is the process of overseeing an organisation. It is about having overall responsibility. This involves ensuring that an organisation's work contributes to its mission and purpose and its resources are used wisely and effectively.

Think of your organisation as a minibus

Who is driving?
Who decides the direction?
Who are the passengers?
What represents the map?

H
Is for... Handling Conflict

Tips for managing conflict
- Acknowledge the conflict
- Try to establish the cause of the conflict
- Develop mutual understanding and respect for difference of opinion
- Identify the need for a solution by all parties

Case study

Good Vibrations is a charity for the benefit of teenagers enabling them to express their issues through music. After a very successful start, the organisation became short of funds and urgently needed a cash injection. The chief officer saw an opportunity to access some funding which would mean the charity would have to work with playgroups as well as teenagers. Because the deadline for the funding was before the next board meeting, he applied for the funding without consulting with the board or staff about the implications. This created a conflict between the board and chief officer over the direction of the organisation and the impact on already overworked volunteers.

1. Discuss the implications of this situation on the future of Good Vibrations?

2. What are some of the potential areas of conflict in our organisation? How can they be avoided?

I

Is for... Information sharing

Make a list of the types of information we use.

Discuss which are the three most important sources of information the board needs to have on a regular basis.

Do we have too much information or not enough?

What different sources of information work best for our board (pictures, video/DVD, presentation, internet, media articles, regular reports)?

Information should be:

Timely – There is no point in having information after it is needed. Information needs to be up to date.

Clear – If information is technical, it should be explained well, so that all board members can understand it.

Concise – If documents are too long, people will not read them. State the facts and keep explanations simple but to the point. Graphs can save space and can encourage board members to understand relationships and engage with the issue better.

Relevant – Only include information that the board needs to know.

Good quality – Make sure facts, and particularly statistics, are based on reliable evidence. Try to include different points of view

J

Is for...
Joining the Board

Cast your mind back to when you came to your first board meeting.

What did you feel? What did you need to know?

Ideas for the perfect induction pack

1. Exciting, colourful folder to carry important documents.
2. A page of photographs of what the organisation does and who is in it.
3. Recent newsletter/publications about the organisation.
4. Role description for being a board member or specific role on the board.
5. List of board members and contact details.
6. List of key dates for the board and key events in the life of the organisation.
7. Copy of recent minutes and annual report.
8. Organisational strategy or business plan.
9. Governing document.
10. Questionnaire about your expectations for being a board member. (to be discussed with the chair in a nice coffee shop/pub)

Is for... Key positions on the board

Characteristics of a good chair – visionary, good at running meetings and getting everyone to contribute, able to handle conflict, good understanding of what the organisation is about, good at summarising discussions and getting people to make decisions.

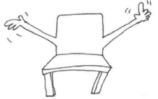

Characteristics of a good secretary – able to summarise the key points, good writing skills, well organised, good at distributing information and following up recommendations from the meetings.

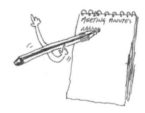

Characteristics of a good treasurer – proven experience in financial management, ability to present financial information in a way that everyone can understand and comment on, well organised, able to meet key deadlines.

Questions

1. Do we agree with these characteristics?
2. What might we want to add?
3. Do these key personnel have role descriptions?
4. Do we have criteria for guiding the selection of board members?

Is for... Liabilities

Trustee liability may arise because of the following reasons:

- Spending charity money on activity outside objects
- Unpermitted political activity
- Fraud
- Serious negligence
- Failing to protect trust property
- Trustee receiving personal benefit
- Acting as trustees or chief officer when disqualified
- Failure to deduct employees' PAYE
- Failure to comply with health and safety, trade descriptions and financial services

Reducing the risk

Here are a few ways of minimising the risks associated with trustee liabilities:

Ensuring the board gets training

Ensuring there are clear roles and responsibilities

Keeping a record of decisions

Regularly reviewing and keeping to the Governing Document

Ensuring good management

Obtaining professional advice

QUESTION
Which of these areas in your organisation is strongest and which does it need to improve in?

A-Z Of Good Governance

M
Is for... Minutes

Minutes are a legal requirement for a registered organisation. They are a record of decisions taken and a reminder of what was discussed at the last meeting, and so can be useful in preparing for the next meeting.

They are also a useful accountability tool for members who agree to carry out a task.

What makes bad minutes?

Minutes are often too detailed. This means the secretary is wasting time and effort when they could be participating more in discussions.

Detailed minutes also make it difficult for board members to find the actions that have been agreed. These could be put in bold or in a separate column.

1. Are our minutes too detailed?
2. Do we keep minutes of every meeting?
3. In what ways could we improve the way we take and store minutes?
4. Do we follow up on action points?

Is for...
The Nolan Principles

Many organisations have found these principles a useful basis for understanding the role of the trustee and they often appear in trustee role descriptions or codes of conduct.

Look at the explanation of the principles on the next page and discuss the extent to which your organisation models these principles.

Selflessness

Decisions are taken solely in terms of public interest, not for personal benefit or financial gain.

Integrity

Trustees should not place themselves under financial or other obligation to outside organisations or individuals that might influence them in the performance of their official duties.

Objectivity

Whether recruiting, awarding contracts, or recommending individuals for rewards or benefits, choices should be made on merit.

Accountability

Trustees are accountable for their decisions to the public and must submit themselves to the appropriate scrutiny.

Openness

Trustees should be open about all decisions and actions, they should give reasons for their decisions and restrict information only when the wider public interest demands.

Honesty

Trustees have a duty to declare any private interests relating to their public duties and to take steps to resolve any conflicts arising in a way that protects the public interest.

Leadership

Trustees should promote and support these principles by leadership and example.

A-Z Of Good Governance

O

Is for... Outcomes

Outcomes are changes that happen as a result of carrying out an activity. Reports to boards often focus on what activities have taken place but may omit details of the results and changes that have happened as a result of the activities.

The role of the board is to look at what has changed as a result of the organisation's activities and how these are helping to fulfil the purpose of the organisation. Information about outcomes can be gathered from questionnaires, interviews, stories of change, and facts and figures from the people the organisation is trying to help.

Make a list of the results you hope to see as a result of your activities.

Which activities are most successful and worth repeating?

Which activities do your staff and volunteers enjoy most?

Have there been any unexpected outcomes as a result of your activities?

A-Z Of Good Governance

P

Is for... Principles of the Code of Governance

The Code of Governance was developed by the National Governance Hub to help trustees lead their organisations and achieve excellent governance.

The main principles of the code are intended to be relevant to all sizes and types of voluntary and community organisations.

How could a Code of Governance help your board?

The 7 Key Principles

1. **Board Leadership** - trustees to collectively ensure delivery of objects, strategic direction and the upholding of values.

2. **The Board in Control** - trustees to be responsible and accountable for ensuring and monitoring that the organisation is performing well, is solvent and complies with its obligations.

3. **The High Performance Board** - trustees should have clear responsibilities and functions, and should organise themselves to discharge them effectively.

4. **Board Review and Renewal** - trustees to periodically review their own and the organisation's effectiveness and take steps to ensure both continue to work well.

5. **Board Delegation** - trustees to set out functions of sub-committees, the chief officer and other staff and monitor their performance.

6. **Board Integrity** - trustees to act according to high ethical standards and deal with conflicts of interest effectively.

7. **The Open Board** - trustees to be accountable to stakeholders.

Is for... Quick team building activities

Traffic light

This is a prescription for improving board effectiveness.

Draw a large traffic light on a flip chart. Then think of your board in terms of behaviours and write by the appropriate coloured light some things the board could consider:

Red - things we could stop doing because they are not helpful to the organisation.

Yellow - things we could start doing because they would help the organisation.

Green - things we could continue doing because they benefit the organisation.

Flipchart Review

To help a board engage in self-examination:

Draw a line down the middle of a flipchart and head one side – "Things we should keep" and the other side "Things we should change".

Board members can then write ideas on post-it notes and stick them on the appropriate side of the chart.

You can group the post-its in order of priority and identify which ones you plan to act on in the short term.

Is for... Review

From time to time, it is important for the board to review how the organisation is doing as a whole. This is an opportunity for the board and staff to ask key questions regarding what is being achieved and what is working well.

Here are three questions which are useful to ask in a review:

1. Do the needs for which the organisation was set up still exist, and is the organisation still meeting these needs?
2. Are these needs being met in the most effective way?
3. How will the results of the review be used to make changes and improvements to the organisation's activities?

Using a timeline to review the work of your organisation

1. Get a long piece of paper (e.g. wallpaper lining)
2. Draw a line, from one end of the paper to the other, which represents the last year in the life of the organisation.
3. In date order, put above the line events or activities that went well, and below the line activities that did not go so well. Illustrate the different activities with cartoons or newspaper cuttings.
4. Discuss and make recommendations for the future.

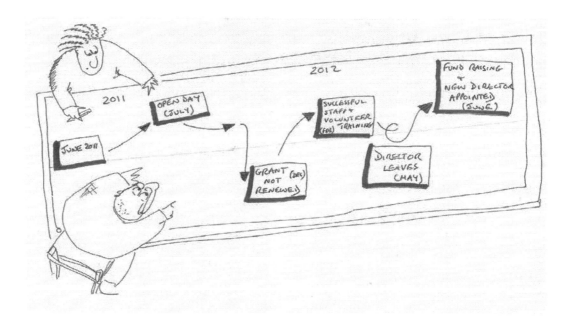

A-Z Of Good Governance

S

Is for... Stakeholders

Make a list of all the people who have an interest in your organisation's work. These are your stakeholders.

Mark beside each person or group of people what their interest is in your organisation.

Discuss who are the different stakeholders and how the organisation is valuing them and communicating with them.

Checklist for working with stakeholders

A stakeholder is someone who has a legitimate interest in your work and the achievements of the organisation. They may include beneficiaries, members, partners, staff, volunteers, regulators and funders. Here is a checklist of things you might like to consider when communicating and consulting with them:

1. Are they kept up to date with the plans and the progress of the organisation?

2. Are they supplied with information in a form they can usefully understand?

3. Are stakeholders' views taken into account when decision making?

4. Is there a procedure for dealing with feedback and complaints from stakeholders?

A-Z Of Good Governance

Is for... Trustees

What are the qualities of a good trustee?
- Committed to the organisation
- Good listening skills
- Contributes to planning the future
- Team player
- Time to give
- Aware of liabilities
- Promotes the organisation

Trustees have 12 main roles

1. Set and maintain vision, mission and values
2. Develop strategy
3. Establish and monitor policies
4. Set up employment procedures
5. Ensure compliance with the Governing Document
6. Ensure accountability
7. Ensure compliance with the law
8. Maintain proper financial oversight
9. Select and support chief executive
10. Respect the role of staff
11. Maintain effective board performance
12. Promote the organisation

In which of these areas do you think your organisation is strong, and in which areas do you think you need to improve?

A-Z Of Good Governance

U

Is for... Useful tips for effective meetings

"The quality of its meetings is a measure of an organisation's effectiveness. Good organisations have good meetings. Good meetings, in turn, make an organisation better."

(from "Common sense for Board members" Edgar Stoesz)

What was the best meeting you ever had, and what made it so?

Ten top tips for effective meetings

1. Provide snacks/nibbles to welcome people to the meeting.
2. Make sure everyone has all the relevant information well in advance.
3. Keep the agenda as short as possible – ideally one piece of paper.
4. Discuss the most important items early in the meeting when participants are most alert.
5. Place a watch or clock in a prominent position so you are able to keep an eye on the time.
6. Remind people of the agenda when they stray away from it.
7. Be selective with information and avoid overload.
8. Encourage members to give their opinions by asking open questions (Why do you think that? What do you think about that? How do you think this can be done?)
9. Write up minutes straight away using notes taken at the meeting.
10. Ask members to give honest feedback on your performance as a chairperson.

V
Is for... Voting

Once the board has spent time discussing an issue, it is necessary to make a decision about the action to be taken.

Each board should choose the way that works best for them whether it be by consensus, majority or unanimity and this should be included in the board manual so everyone knows how the system works.

Often the vote will be for or against a proposal, or board members could vote for one option from a number of choices:

- Approve the action proposed
- Approve the action with amendments
- Reject the action
- Ask for more information to be provided

Questions

1. How good is our board at making decisions?
2. Would it be helpful for us to agree rules of debate?
3. How can we improve our decision-making processes?
4. Do the members have enough information to help them make their decisions?

Is for... Working within your objects

"Objects" is the term we use to describe and identify the purposes for which the organisation has been set up and it is the board's responsibility to ensure the organisation sticks to these. The objects should be stated in the Governing Document.

It may be tempting to stray from the original objects for various reasons - maybe because of personal aspirations, or you may be looking for new opportunities which could bring in much needed funding. (see case study for 'Handling Conflict') However, the implications of doing so can result in legal and financial problems for the organisation.

Questions

1. Are all board members aware of the objects of the organisation?
2. Do we have regular reviews to make sure the organisation is keeping to its objects?
3. What are the factors that may cause us to stray from our objects?

A-Z Of Good Governance

X Is for... eXperts

Even the most qualified committee may need financial, legal or technical advice to help them make good decisions. There are plenty of organisations out there, whose job it is to help you. The Code of Good Governance lists these organisations.

Some of the main ones are listed on the next page:

1. Make a list of the areas in which you think you might need expert advice.
2. Prioritise the areas which need most attention.
3. Agree who will contact the appropriate expert or organisation and by when.

Organisations that can assist trustees

Charities Evaluation Services
www.ces-vol.org.uk
0207 713 5722

Charity Commission
www.charity-commission.gov.uk
0845 300 0218

Black Training and Enterprise Group
www.bteg.co.uk
0207 832 5800

Community Matters
www.communitymatters.org.uk
0207 837 7887

Institute of Fundraising
www.institute-of-fundraising.org.uk
0207 840 1000

Volunteering England
www.volunteering.org.uk
0207 520 8900

National Council for Voluntary Organisations
www.ncvo-vol.org.uk
0207 713 6161

Y

Is for... Young people

Youth is no bar to being an effective trustee. Young people may lack experience, but can bring energy, creativity and enthusiasm to a board, and therefore have an important part to play.

It is especially important for organisations who exist for the benefit of young people to have young people involved in their decision making process.

And it's a two way thing – the organisation benefits and so do the young people. For some still involved in full time education it is a fantastic opportunity. Having a role in making long-term decisions about a voluntary organisation can create skills that are directly transferable to paid work.

Questions

1. Are young people represented on our board?
2. What are the strengths of the young people on the board?
3. Are the views of young people listened to?
4. How can we get more young people involved?

A-Z Of Good Governance

Is for... Zeal

Keeping your trustees, staff and volunteers motivated is key to achieving what you want to do.

It is important to think of different ways of keeping people motivated and inspired, whether they have just joined the organisation or been there for some years.

Think about what motivates the people in your organisation.

How can you build on this to meet their needs and the needs of the organisation?

6 top tips for keeping trustees, staff and volunteers motivated

1. Identify and use skills and experience.
2. Recognise achievements and celebrate them.
3. Involve people in discussions and future plans.
4. Provide training and support when appropriate.
5. Create a sense of belonging.
6. Make your organisation a rewarding and fun place to be.

A-Z Of Good Governance

Suggested publications

Good Governance: A practical guide for boards, chairs and CEOs

Dorothy Dalton: NCVO
www.ncvo-vol.org.uk

Good Trustee Guide

Peter Dyer
Dorothy Dalton: NCVO
www.ncvo-vol.org.uk

Common sense for Board members

Edgar Stoesz. Good books
www.goodbks.com

A-Z Of Good Governance

Final thoughts

Quotes from Common sense for Board members by Edgar Stoesz

"Board service is like jazz - you experiment until you find a chord that works, and then you play it for all you can. Board service is frequently an exercise in creative pragmatism."

"All boards face a common temptation - spending too much time on administrative detail. They tend to control instead of lead."

A-Z Of Good Governance

"Where there is no vision, the people perish."

Proverbs 29:18

"The next time staff present your board with an impressive list of activities, ask in a simple and sincere way, 'So what?' What difference did it/will it make? Board work is about outcomes, not about activities."

A-Z Of Good Governance

About Mosaic Creative

We are a small training consultancy, working mainly in the field of community development, both in the UK and internationally, specialising in the use of drama, cartoons and illustrations to enhance learning and development.

Our approach is about provoking a reaction, communicating ideas, exploring meaning and unlocking the creative potential in others. Mosaic Creative has an in house capacity to design and produce its own publications as well as tailor-made resources for clients.

Bill Crooks

Bill has worked with the not for profit sector for over 25 years, both in the UK and internationally, running courses on a wide range of community development issues. He is an accomplished cartoonist and illustrator and uses these skills to powerful effect in his training courses and workshops. This includes the use of graphic facilitation for capturing learning from conferences and strategic events. He has written and illustrated many community development resources, currently being used in the UK and internationally.

Jackie Mouradian

Jackie is a professional actor, script writer and facilitator, working with both the corporate and charity sectors, especially in the context of organisational change and development. She writes and performs in sketches relevant to the needs of the company or organisation and provides meaningful and realistic environments within which effective learning can take place. She also co-writes community development resources for use in the UK and internationally.

Lindsay Noble

Lindsay's graphic design work at Mosaic Creative focuses on developing accessible, user-friendly and exciting designs for resource materials used in a variety of cross cultural settings.

For further details, please contact:

info@mosaiccreative.co.uk
www.mosaiccreative.co.uk

Printed in Great Britain
by Amazon.co.uk, Ltd.,
Marston Gate.